# Carving Water Birds

## Patterns and Instructions for 12 Models

### by
### ANTHONY HILLMAN

Dover Publications, Inc., New York

Published in Canada by General Publishing Company, Ltd., 30 Lesmill Road, Don Mills, Toronto, Ontario.
Published in the United Kingdom by Constable and Company, Ltd., 3 The Lanchesters, 162–164 Fulham Palace Road, London W6 9ER.

*Carving Water Birds: Patterns and Instructions for 12 Models* is a new work, first published by Dover Publications, Inc., in 1990.

Manufactured in the United States of America
Dover Publications, Inc., 31 East 2nd Street, Mineola, N.Y. 11501

**Library of Congress Cataloging in Publication Data**

Hillman, Anthony
    Carving water birds : patterns and instructions for 12 models / by Anthony Hillman.
        p.     cm.
    ISBN 0-486-26505-6
    1. Water birds in art.   2. Wood-carving — Technique.   I. Title.
    NK9704.H55    1990                                              90-44802
                                                                            CIP

# HOW TO CARVE A WATER BIRD

There is no bird more frequently associated with northern lakes than the Common Loon, with the southern seacoast than the Brown Pelican or with shore settings anywhere in North America than the Herring Gull. This book includes patterns for carving these three familiar birds as well as nine others associated with water — birds of rivers, lakes, wetlands and the seashore. All twelve are different, and all make for interesting, highly unusual bird carvings. Six of the carvings are life-size and, for the other six, the actual size of each bird is given for those who want to enlarge the patterns (space limitations here prohibit providing full-size patterns for very large birds such as the Brown Pelican and Great Blue Heron).

The patterns for these water-bird carvings are of several types. Seven must be carved from two separate pieces of wood, one each for the head and body. The templates for these have been drawn showing the heads and bodies joined to provide a full picture of the birds, and so that the patterns can be used for purposes other than carving. When used for carving, the head and body templates should be cut out and mounted separately.

Each of the other five carvings may be made from a single piece of wood at the scale of the templates (two, the Common Tern and the Virginia Rail, are life-size). Four of the carvings are of "floating" birds — made as if the bird were floating on a body of water, with only the parts normally above the waterline showing. The other carvings show the birds standing, walking (Virginia Rail) or perched (Kingfisher; this may also be done standing, as on the inside cover). As three of these are life-size, you may obtain cast feet for these, avoiding the difficult task of creating convincing replicas of the birds' feet. Since it is often difficult to find proper cast feet for other than life-size models, I have given below instructions for making feet out of wire and toothpicks.

Study the patterns before you begin any work. Yet another point: while the profile patterns may always be cut out and used as templates, as well as the top view of the body in most cases (only half of this may be given; simply flip over this piece to trace the other half onto the wood), the top and front views of the head cannot be used in this way and are intended for reference only. And finally, for each carving I have specified the *minimum-size* pieces of dressed wood required. When in doubt always use larger pieces; these of course can be readily cut down if necessary. Many types of wood suitable for carving are available locally. Obtain the best clear, straight-grained wood available in your area. And remember — always place the direction of the grain to run with the longest dimension of the piece to be carved.

Now remove the staples and spread the pages out flat. Select the plates with the patterns for the projects you wish to carve. You can cut out the patterns and use them directly as templates, but I recommend that you give them permanence by gluing them to $^3/_{16}''$ mahogany exterior plywood. Mahogany is recommended because even pieces as thin as these will be durable. Carefully recut the patterns. Varnish will seal the edges. Mounting the patterns in this manner will preserve them for making duplicates. On the head template, drill a hole in the eye big enough for marking eye position. (Remember not to mount the top- or front-view patterns! These are for reference only.)

Read completely through the following instructions before taking any steps to begin carving. We will use the Great Blue Heron as an example. This large wading bird is found throughout most of the continental United States and Canada, often seen feeding in shallow water or flying majestically overhead. I recommend using basswood for this somewhat "tender" carving. Its fine, almost invisible grain is ideal for the curves found in this pattern. Cut out the profile patterns for the body and the head position of your choice, and prepare them for use as templates. Begin carving procedures with the head.

## THE HEAD

As a general rule, the head of your carving will demand more time and effort than the body. Generally, what you want to achieve in your carving, especially of the head, is symmetry of form. In other words, the eyes should be opposite each other! Also, both cheeks should be equally rounded, and the neck and top of the head should have the same graceful curves on either side. Many superdetailed decorative carvings are spoiled simply because of unevenness in the basic carving.

Using a piece of wood of the specified dimensions, lay the template for the head so that the grain runs *with the bill* (see Figure 1). With a band saw, cut carefully around the outline. If you are using the head pattern with the very sharp curve under the neck (upper left on Plate 12), you may prevent the band saw from binding in the curve by predrilling this area using a ¼″ bit.

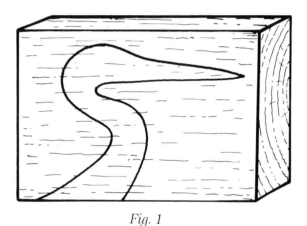

*Fig. 1*

Now take the sawn-out piece of wood and measure the half-thickness of your stock. With a pencil, mark down the middle of the entire head block on all sawn surfaces. *Never cut this line away!* It is the cross section of the head and should be there when you finish-sand your carving.

At this point you may want to drill guide holes for the eyes, while the sides of the head are flat. Use a drill press if available.

Next, taper the sides of the head from top to bottom. Whittle this taper with a knife. Keep checking both sides (Fig. 2).

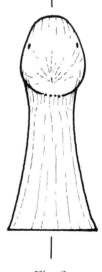

*Fig. 2*

Look at the head from the top. Make sure that the cross-section line remains clearly marked. Using the profile pattern as a guide, mark a line across the upper side of the bill, perpendicular to the cross-section line, indicating where the top of the bill ends (see also the top-view pattern for position). Mark another line across where the underside of the bill ends, corresponding to the line just made above, also perpendicular to the cross-section line. On carvings with sharply pointed bill tips, do not carve all the way down to the sharp point; always leave a little extra thickness so the final shape can be achieved by sandpapering. Refer to the top and side views of the head. Whether you carve the bill first or last is a matter of personal preference. You can mark the cuts for bill width and then start at the neck. The heron, of course, has quite a neck to carve! Follow the patterns for taper, and don't forget to mark the centerline on all surfaces of the head and neck. On the base of the neck draw an oval touching all four edges (and the points at which the centerline meets the edges). This marks the outline of the neck where it joins the body.

Now you can carve off the corners of the neck and make it nice and round. Also round out the shape of the head. When you have carved the head and neck to your satisfaction, carefully sand with #80 sandpaper. Drill holes for the eyes and glue them in. The nostrils and the margins of the bill may be painted in (you may wait until you paint the entire carving), cut in (do this before the final sanding) or burned in with a wood-burning tool (pyroelectric pen). (Do not do any wood burning, however, until you have finish-sanded the carving.) When carving, if you grasp the head or neck as close as you comfortably can to the area you are carving, this will greatly minimize the chance of snapping the neck. If you should accidentally damage the bill, you can still save the neck: simply saw off the remainder of the bill, drill a hole, glue in a dowel of the right thickness, and recarve.

## THE BODY

Be sure to use a piece of wood that is large enough and has the grain running along its length. Using the body template, saw out the shape with a band saw (Fig. 3). Be sure that the place where the head goes is perfectly flat. As with

*(Instructions continue after Plates.)*

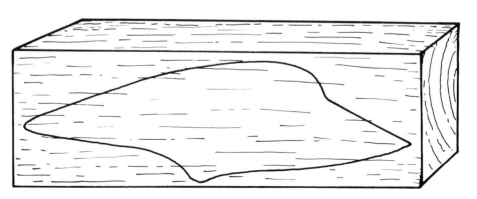

*Fig. 3*

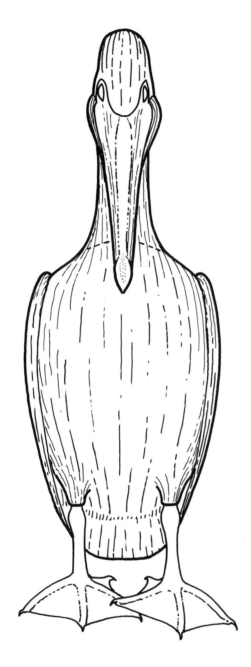

FRONT VIEW

TOP VIEW

# Brown Pelican

Whether dramatically plunging into the water for fish or just perched
on an old piling, the Brown Pelican may be seen almost anywhere
along the coast of Florida and the Gulf of Mexico and along much of
the southeast and southwest coasts as well.

Plate 1 *(left)*

Remove staples to see and use full patterns.

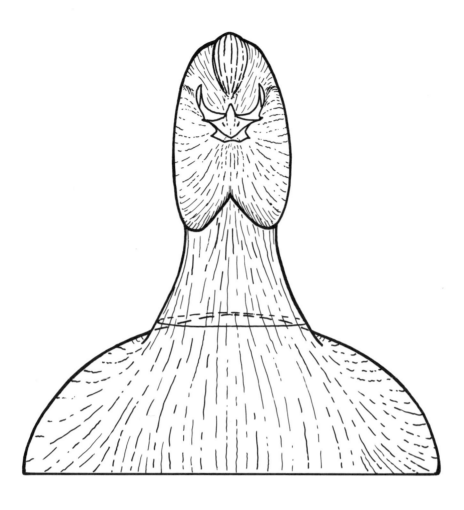

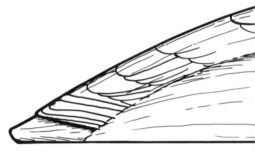

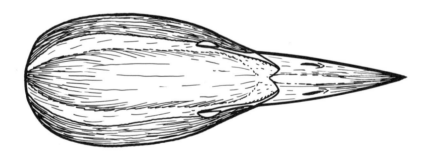

TOP VIEW

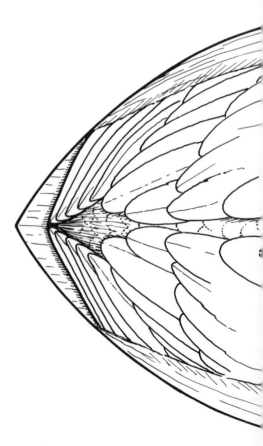

# Horned Grebe

Grebes, like loons, are thoroughly adapted to life in the water and are rarely seen in the air or on land. The Horned Grebe nests on small bodies of water on the northern prairies of the U.S. and Canada. In the winter it is seen primarily offshore on East, West and Gulf coasts. It dives for small fish and other creatures.

Plate 2 *(left)*

# Black Skimmer

Skimmers, though closely related to the terns, are unique: no other birds have a lower mandible that is longer than the upper. Skimmers do what their name suggests: they fly very low over a body of water, dipping their lower mandible into the water to detect small fish and other creatures, which they then seize and eat. The Black Skimmer, found primarily along the Atlantic and Gulf coasts, is one of three species of skimmers, the other two inhabiting Africa and India, respectively.

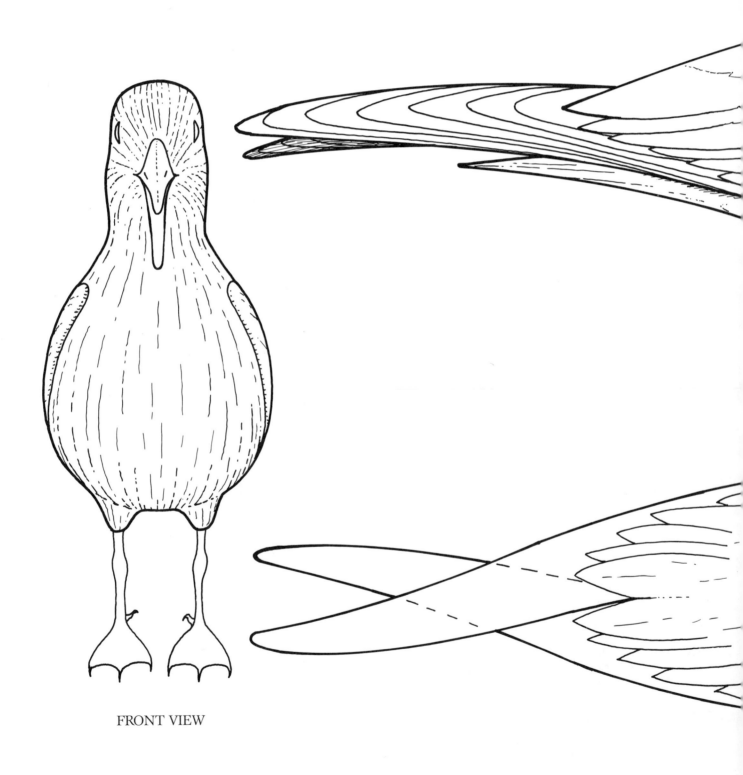

FRONT VIEW

Plate 3 *(left)*

Remove staples to see and use full patterns.

TOP VIEW          FRONT VIEW

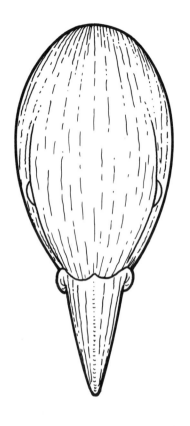

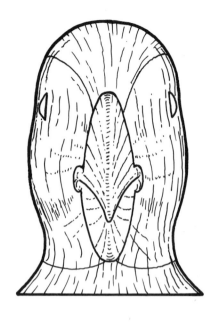

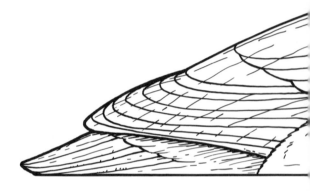

# Atlantic Puffin

Probably more people have seen this unusual seabird in
zoos than in the wild, for in North America it nests only off
the coast of Maine and of eastern Canada. Able to keep the
mandibles of their colorful bills parallel when opened,
puffins can this way carry several small fish at once.

Minimum Size Dressed Wood Required (life-size)
Body: 9½″ long × 2¼″ deep × 5″ wide
Head: 4½″ long × 3″ deep × 2″ wide
Eyes: 8mm gray

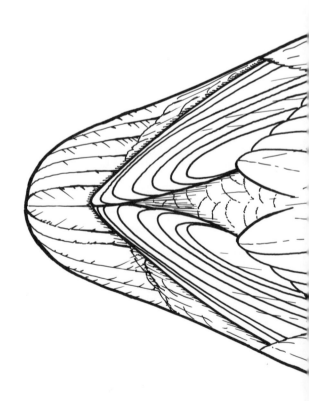

Plate 4 *(left)*

Remove staples to see and use full patterns.

# Common Tern

This graceful, delicate-looking bird dives for fish from high in the air. It may appear over any North American coastal waters during migration, and in the summer is conspicuous around its breeding grounds in the northeast and central U.S. and in much of Canada.

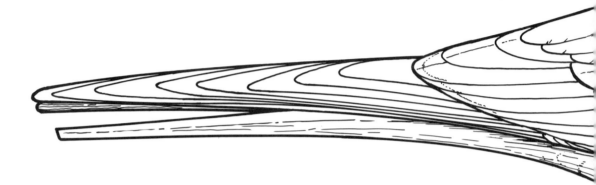

Minimum Size Dressed Wood Required (life-size)
Body and head: 13½″ long × 4½″ deep × 2¾″ wide
Eyes: 6mm black or dark brown

Notes: I recommend a fine-grained stock, such as basswood, for this carving.

Trim tail *carefully* from underside, paying attention to direction of grain. If desired, the cuts separating tail and wings may be eliminated to strengthen this fragile area.

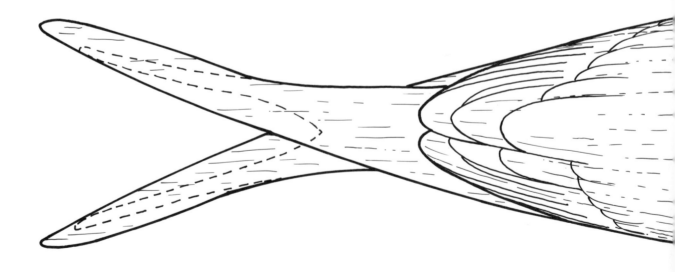

Plate 5 *(left)*

Remove staples to see and use full patterns.

# American Coot

Though they swim and dive like ducks and look a little like chickens, coots are in fact related to the rails. Far less secretive than any rail, however, the American Coot may be seen in and around water — especially ponds and marshes — almost anywhere in North America.

Minimum Size Dressed Wood Required (life-size)
Body: 10½″ long × 2½″ deep × 5½″ wide
Head: 4″ long × 3¾″ deep × 1¾″ wide
Eyes: 8mm red

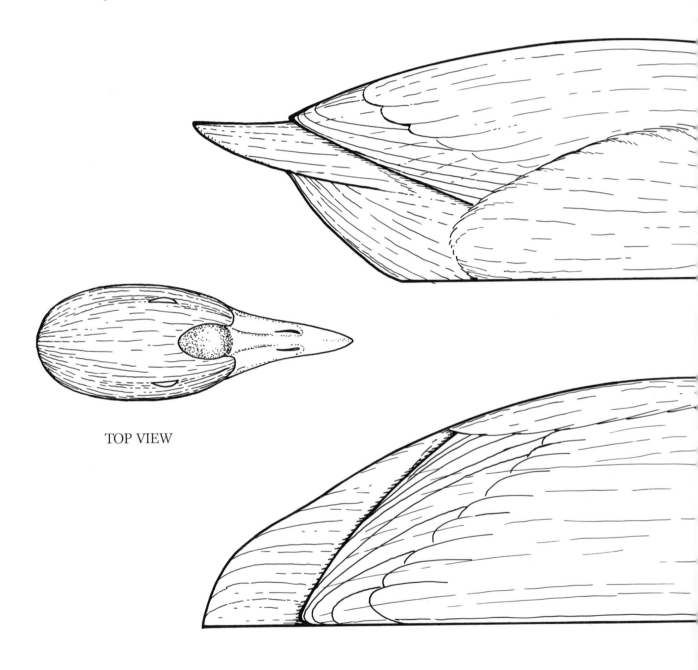

TOP VIEW

Plate 6 *(left)*

Remove staples to see and use full patterns.

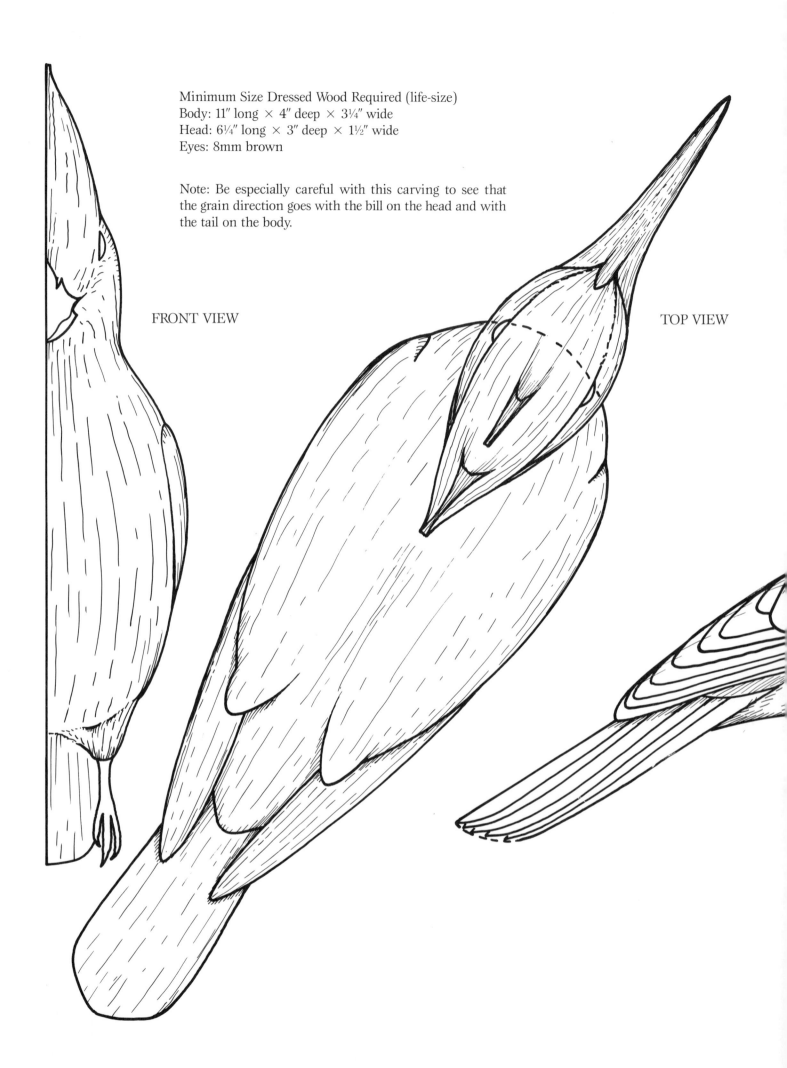

Minimum Size Dressed Wood Required (life-size)
Body: 11″ long × 4″ deep × 3¼″ wide
Head: 6¼″ long × 3″ deep × 1½″ wide
Eyes: 8mm brown

Note: Be especially careful with this carving to see that
the grain direction goes with the bill on the head and with
the tail on the body.

FRONT VIEW

TOP VIEW

Plate 7 *(left)*

# Common Loon

This handsome green, black and white diving bird is the only loon
that breeds in any of the lower 48 states, though only in the far north,
as well as in Canada. It is also the only loon that winters on all parts of
the Atlantic, Pacific and Gulf coasts.

TOP VIEW

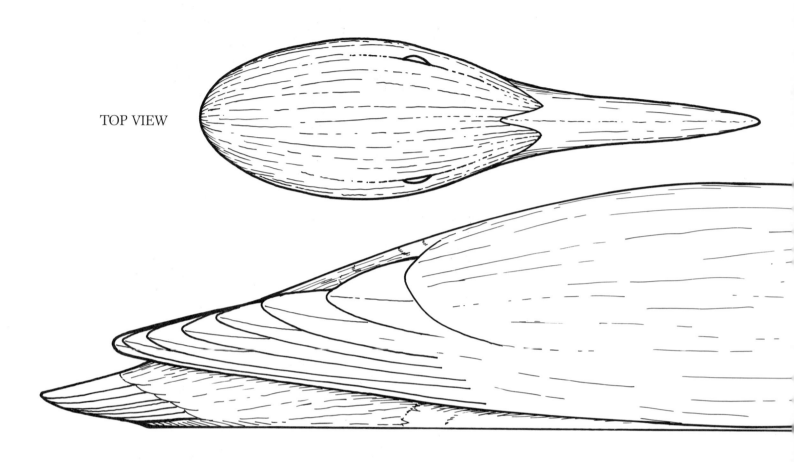

Minimum Size Dressed Wood Required at This Scale
Body: 15½″ long × 2¾″ deep × 6¾″ wide
Head: 6½″ long × 3½″ deep × 2″ wide
Eyes: 8mm red
Actual length of live bird: 24″

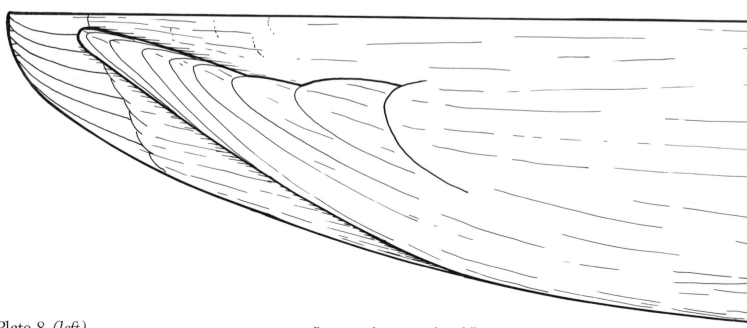

Plate 8 *(left)*

Remove staples to see and use full patterns.

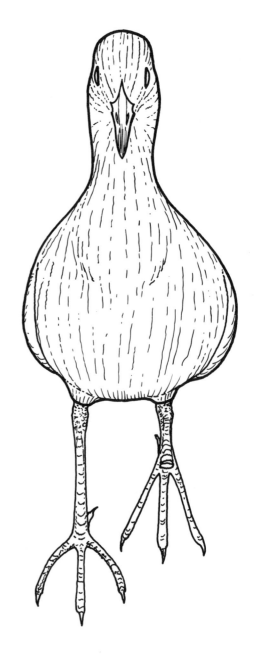

FRONT VIEW

# Virginia Rail

This widespread inhabitant of reedy places in marshes is common, but, like all rails, secretive and hard to see.

Minimum Size Dressed Wood Required (life-size)
Body and head: 9″ long × 4″ deep × 2½″ wide
Eyes: 6mm brown

Plate 9 *(left)*

TOP VIEW

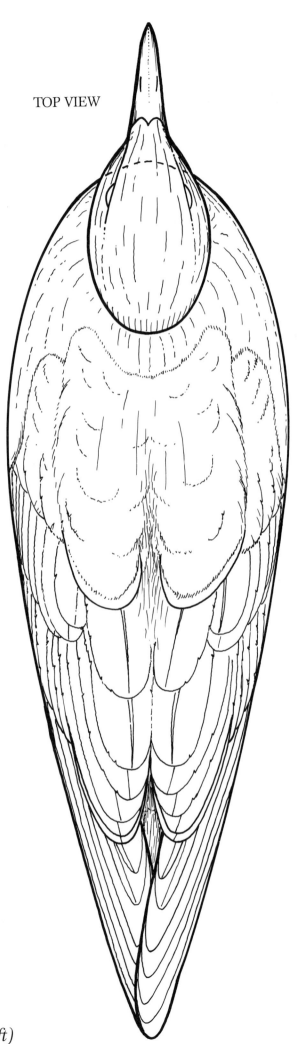

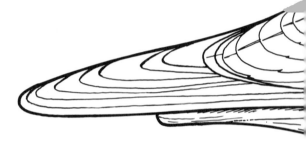

# Herring Gull

If you spot a "sea gull" near the docks, a landfill or a river, there is a good chance that it is this widespread gull, which breeds as far north as the shore of the Arctic Ocean and winters as far south as Mexico's Yucatán peninsula (it is also found in Europe and Asia).

Plate 10 *(left)*

TOP VIEW

# Glossy Ibis

Once confined to the Old World, this exotic-looking marsh dweller has extended its range on its own so that it is now found all along the East Coast of the U.S. A similar species, the White-faced Ibis, inhabits much of the West.

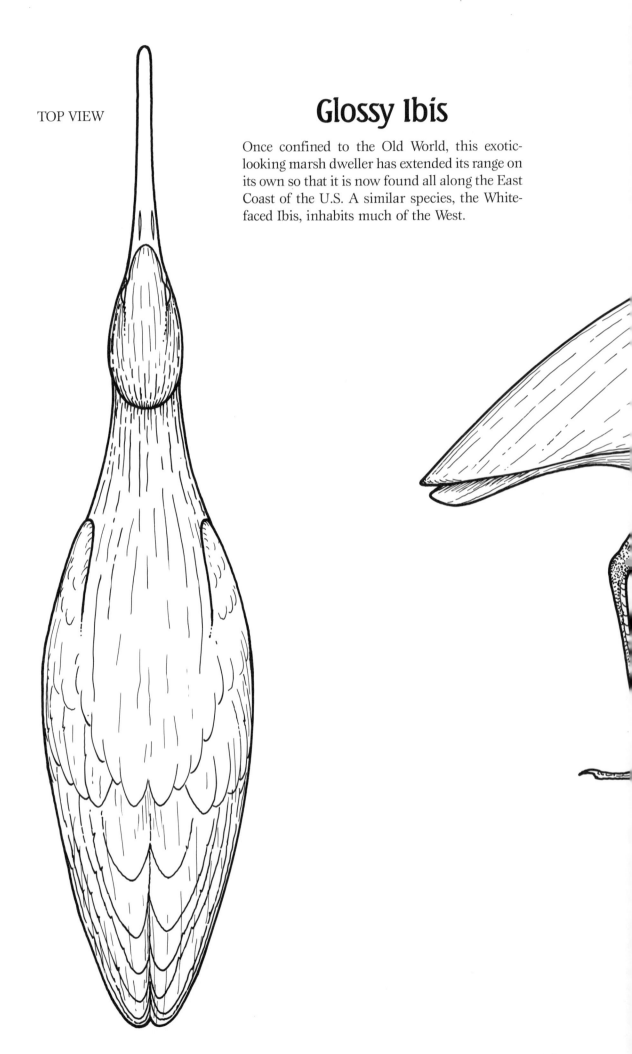

Plate 11 *(left)*

Remove staples to see and use full patterns.

# Great Blue Heron

This largest North American heron is an elegant wading bird that may be seen stalking fish in the shallow water of lakes and marshes almost anywhere from coast to coast.

Plate 12 *(left)*

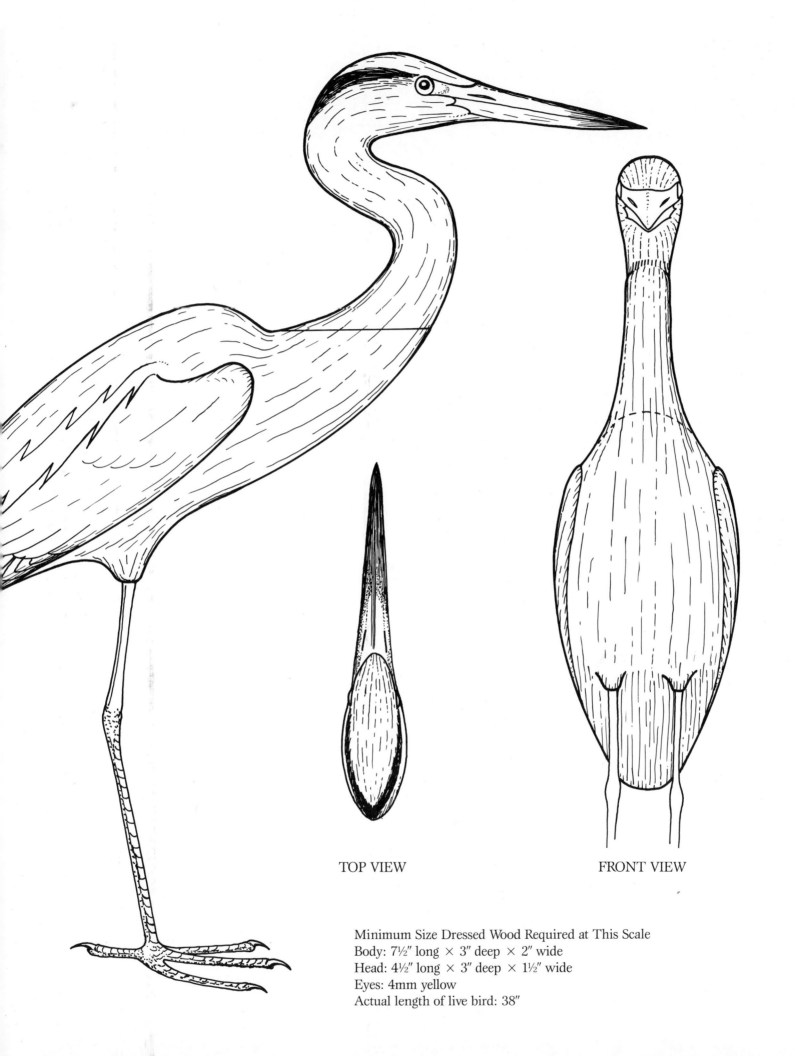

TOP VIEW

FRONT VIEW

Minimum Size Dressed Wood Required at This Scale
Body: 7½″ long × 3″ deep × 2″ wide
Head: 4½″ long × 3″ deep × 1½″ wide
Eyes: 4mm yellow
Actual length of live bird: 38″

Remove staples to see and use full patterns.

Plate 12 *(right)*

Minimum Size Dressed Wood Required at This Scale
Body and head: 10½″ long × 5″ deep × 2⅜″ wide
Eyes: 5mm brown
Actual length of live bird: 19″

FRONT VIEW

Plate 11 *(right)*

Minimum Size Dressed Wood Required at This Scale
Body and head: 11″ long × 5¾″ deep × 3⅛″ wide
Eyes: 8 mm yellow or straw
Actual length of live bird: 20″

FRONT VIEW

TOP VIEW

Plate 9 *(right)*

TOP VIEW

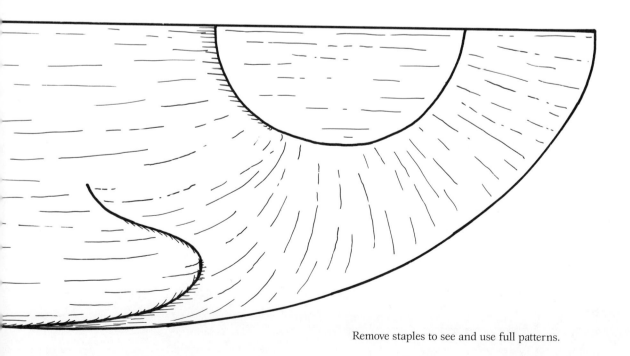

Remove staples to see and use full patterns.

Plate 8 *(right)*

# Belted Kingfisher

The sole representative in most of North America of a large, colorful worldwide family, the Belted Kingfisher can turn up almost anywhere around water in the U.S. or Canada. Like terns and Brown Pelicans (though totally unrelated to either) kingfishers plunge dramatically into the water to catch fish. The female (seen here) is slightly more colorful than the male, having a rusty belly band in addition to the gray-blue and white markings shared by both sexes.

FRONT VIEW

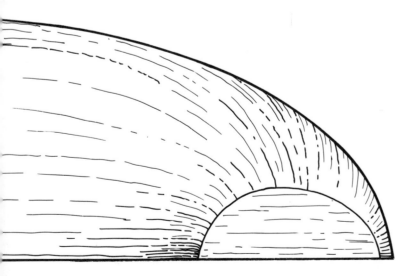

TOP VIEW

Plate 6 *(right)*

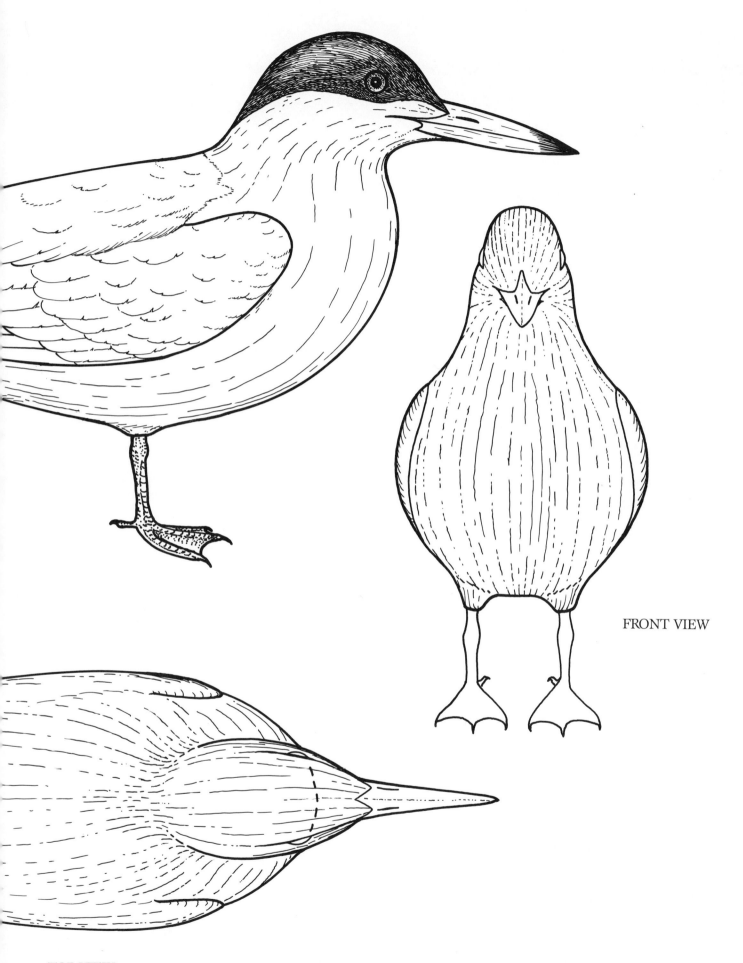

FRONT VIEW

TOP VIEW

Plate 5 *(right)*

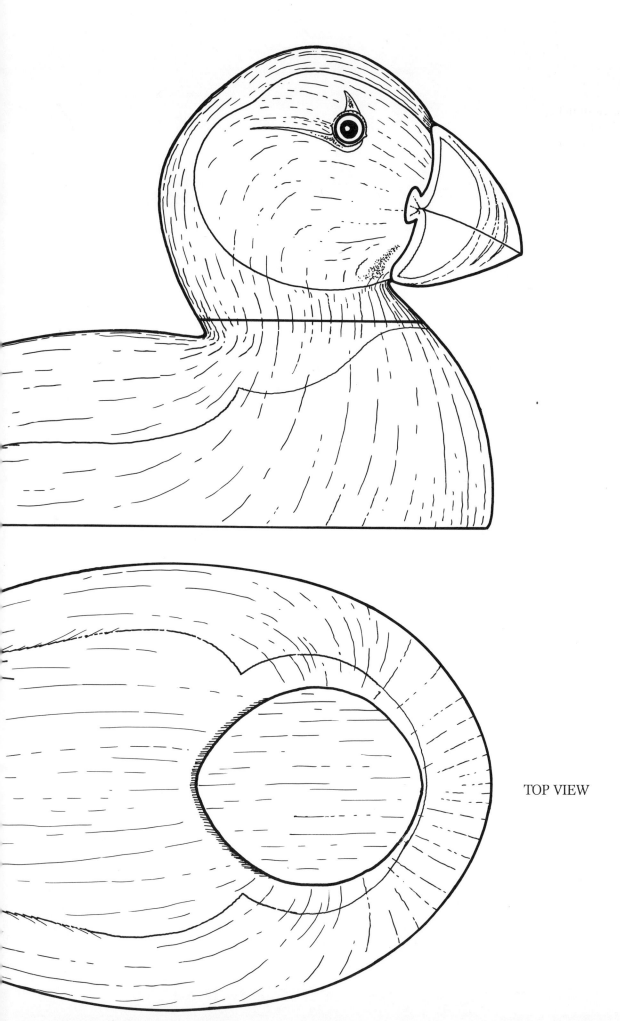

TOP VIEW

Remove staples to see and use full patterns.

Plate 4 *(right)*

Minimum Size Dressed Wood Required at This Scale
Body and head: 14″ long × 5¼″ deep × 3″ wide
Eyes: 6mm brown
Actual length of live bird: 17″

TOP VIEW

Plate 3 *(right)*

Minimum Size Dressed Wood Required (life-size)
Body: 9¼″ long × 1¾″ deep × 5″ wide
Head: 4½″ long × 3¼″ deep × 1¾″ wide
Eyes: 6mm red

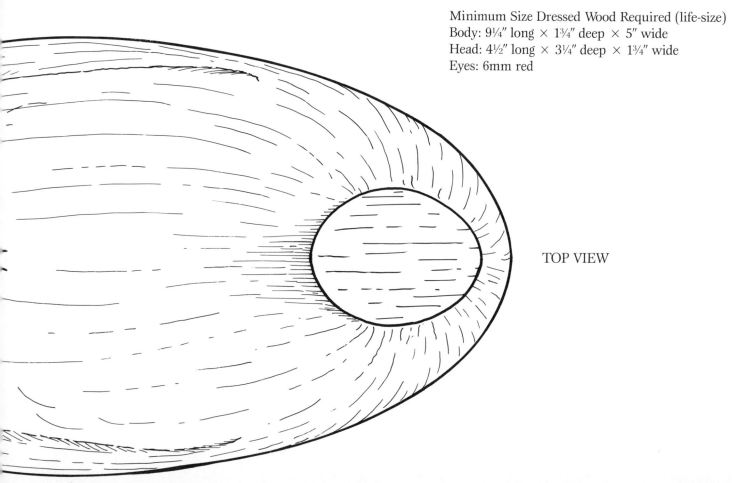

TOP VIEW

Plate 2 *(right)*

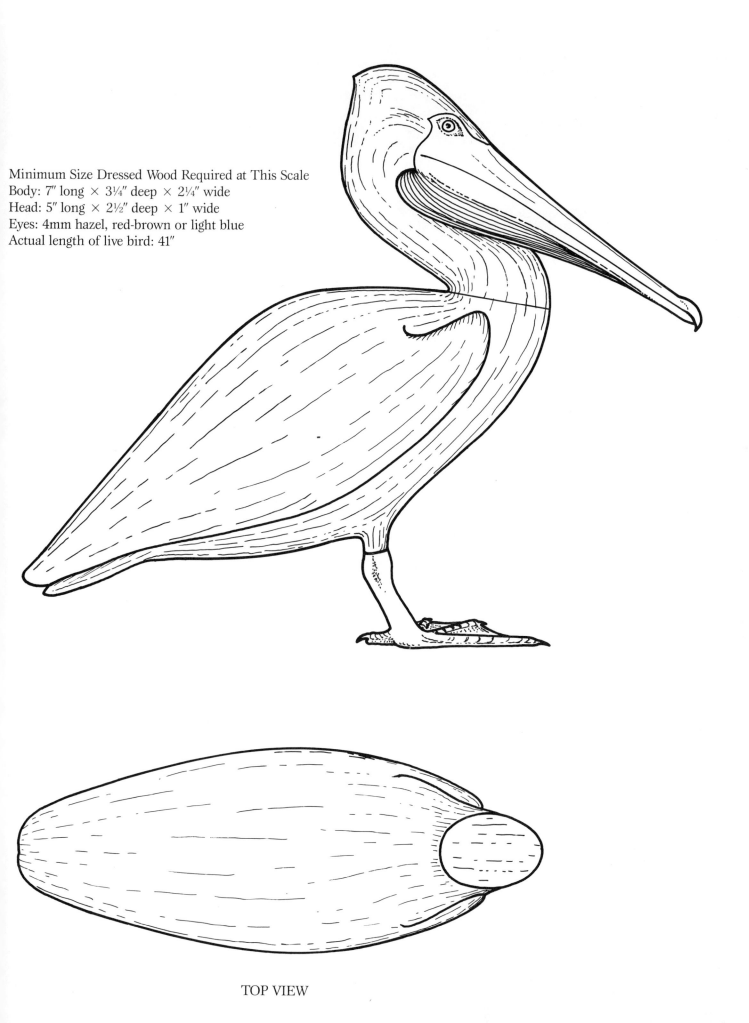

Minimum Size Dressed Wood Required at This Scale
Body: 7″ long × 3¼″ deep × 2¼″ wide
Head: 5″ long × 2½″ deep × 1″ wide
Eyes: 4mm hazel, red-brown or light blue
Actual length of live bird: 41″

TOP VIEW

Plate 1 *(right)*

the head, measure the half-thickness and draw a centerline in pencil all around the piece of wood. Also, mark the position of the legs. Next place the base of the neck on the flat surface precisely where it will be attached to the body. Draw a line completely around it to mark the spot exactly. Begin to carve by working from the middle outward. Remember not to cut away the centerline! Use the front-view pattern as a guide. Taper the shape around the breast and up to the neck joint. Mark the wings and carve these in relief (these may be simply painted if you desire a simpler carving project). The area where the legs will be inserted should be carved so as to bulge slightly relative to the surrounding area. Finish carving around the entire body. When this has been done to your satisfaction, glue the head in place. If the joint between head and body is not smooth, simply fair the neck into the body with your knife *after the glue in the joint is thoroughly dry.* (Note: if you enlarge these patterns to carve a larger bird, you should secure the head to the body with a couple of finishing nails in addition to the glue.) Now sand the body with #80 sandpaper. Finish-sand the entire carving with #220 or finer sandpaper. If you wish, you may now add feather detail by wood burning (always do this after finish-sanding, or you will undo your work and clog the fine carving details with wood dust).

## ADDING FEET

Carving convincing birds' legs is not an easy task. Beginners will probably want to purchase cast feet (most of what we think of as "legs" on most birds are actually feet, so I will generally refer to the legs and feet as simply "feet" from now on) and insert them. It may be wise to do this in any case since unrealistic, poorly constructed feet can really destroy the appearance of an otherwise outstanding work. One problem that arises when carving at less than life size is that cast feet may not be available at that scale. I was able to obtain miniature cast feet for the Brown Pelican and several other species from Ritter Carvers of Maple Glen, Pennsylvania. Another good source of cast feet (as well as glass eyes) is the Christian J. Hummul Company of Easton, Maryland (the addresses of these mail-order suppliers are given below).

Another method of creating accurate replicas of birds' feet is to carve them using the cast feet for reference. This way you can scale the feet down to the size of your carving.

There is yet another method of dealing with the feet. On the Virginia Rail I found it difficult to bend the cast feet to the positions I wanted. I solved this problem by carving wooden dowels for all but the toes and then sawing off the toes of the store-bought feet and gluing them, bent into the position I wanted, to the carved dowels (I used a hot-melt glue). As may be seen on the front cover, the problem of carving accurate feet may be satisfactorily avoided altogether by simply substituting simple wire legs inserted into a base. For the Great Blue Heron I used the wire from an ordinary clothes hanger! Any brass rod or wire of a suitable thickness will do, bent at the appropriate angle in the right place. Pay close attention to the angle at which the legs will enter the body and then drill the holes. You may have a

problem, as I did, finding the right size drill bit for this. The problem may be solved by using a piece of the wire itself as the drill bit! Cut a length of about 3″ of your wire stock, create a sharp point and use this as you would any regular drill bit. This method usually makes a tight fit. Glue the wire into the body, and bend the wire at the proper distance from the body. You can make the points where the legs go into the base by pressing the ends into the wood to make slight indentations. Again, pay close attention to the angle of entry into the base; then drill the holes. Be sure to allow enough wire in the legs so after one end has been inserted into the body and the other into the base there is enough left showing. You may glue the legs into the base if you wish.

Finally I might mention yet another alternative in creating feet: using toothpicks for toes. These are used in addition to wire. The toothpicks are cut to the proper length and used in combination to suggest jointed parts of toes. Glue them to the base radiating outward from the leg wires (Fig. 4).

You may find some of these procedures a bit tricky at first, but as with any activity, they will become easier with practice. Before long you will find that you too will be enjoying giving a bit of life to a piece of wood as you become more proficient in your carving!

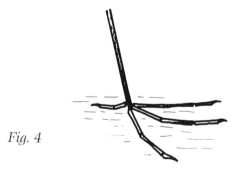

*Fig. 4*

## FINISHING YOUR CARVING

Generally the next step is to apply paint, but some hobbyists prefer to give their carvings a natural finish instead. If this is your intention, it is very important to give your work an extremely fine sanding (*before* wood burning!). Then, after sanding and any wood burning you may wish to do, apply varnish or shellac as desired. You may also consider staining the wood; just proceed as above and apply the stain before you apply the varnish or shellac. Remember to follow the instructions found on the labels of the products you use. Take special care to observe all safety precautions when working with volatile or toxic substances.

Most likely you will want to paint your carving in natural colors. To do so, prime it with three coats of gesso diluted to a thin wash. (Ordinary paint primer is satisfactory if your carving has little or no feather detail.) Allow for complete drying between coats. Once the wood has been thus coated, you are free to use sandpaper once more. It may be necessary to sand at this point if the primer raises the grain of the wood. If you do so, be sure to remove all of the resulting dust, or it may clog the feather detail. Now you are ready to paint your carving.

There are many different ways of painting wildlife carvings. What I offer here is a few basic procedures as an example. Before any actual painting, gather as many sources as you can that show the coloration of the species you are representing. Try to observe living birds whenever possible. This is not as difficult as it may sound. True, a few of the birds in this book are restricted in their range, like the Atlantic Puffin (coastal extreme northeast U.S. and Canada) and the Brown Pelican (primarily southeast, southwest and Gulf coasts); but many — the Great Blue Heron is a good example — are familiar, widely distributed species; and a few, like the Herring Gull, may turn up almost anywhere and are abundant even in some of our most urbanized areas. I caution against just collecting photographs and other images without firsthand observation. Certain subtle aspects of form and color cannot be properly appreciated except in the living creatures themselves. Close study of these subtleties is therefore important, but it is also fun. With practice and observation, you will gradually find it becoming easier to paint realistically (naturally, that goes for carving as well).

When you have primed your carving and the primer or gesso has dried, lightly mark in pencil the borders of the main areas of color. Now you are ready to paint. The question of whether to use oil or acrylic paint must be faced. Acrylics are more popular and are recommended for the beginner because they dry quickly and allow brushes to be cleaned with soap and water. Just remember to use an oil-base primer under oil paint, and an acrylic primer under acrylic paint.

Apply large, basic areas of color first. Also, as a rule, apply light colors first, then darker. If you let the paint dry, you can then use a dry-brush technique to stipple on feathers. If you wish colors to blend into each other with no discernible edges, use a wet-on-wet technique. Always remember to study the color photographs on the covers, as well as your other reference sources and, of course, live birds wherever possible. Gradually you will refine your technique. With practice and patience you will even be able to give the feathers a look of fluffiness.

## A NOTE ON SUPPLIERS

You may be able to buy such items as wood-burning tools, glass eyes and cast feet where you obtain your woodcarving and painting tools and materials. Check your local classified telephone directory. The following mail-order suppliers carry stocks of glass eyes and cast feet. It is a good idea to write or telephone for information before ordering.

Christian J. Hummul Co., Inc.
404 Brookletts Avenue
P.O. Box 1849
Easton, MD 21601
Telephone: (301) 820-8760

Ritter Carvers
William Ritter
1559 Dillon Road
Maple Glen, PA 19002
Telephone (after 5 P.M.): (215) 646-4896